WRITTEN BY
DOMINIQUE JOLY, DORINE BARBEY, ALAIN DUPAS,
BRIGITTE GANDIOL-COPPIN, CATHERINE DE LASA, GENEVIÈVE LAURENCIN,
ODILE LIMOUSIN, DANIÈLE NEUMANN, FRÉDÉRIQUE THIOLLIER

COVER DESIGN BY
STEPHANIE BLUMENTHAL

TRANSLATED AND ADAPTED BY
ROBERT NEUMILLER

PUBLISHED BY CREATIVE EDUCATION
123 South Broad Street, Mankato, Minnesota 56001
Creative Education is an imprint of The Creative Company

Library of Congress Cataloging-in-Publication Data
[Les métiers des hommes. English]
People at Work / by Dominique Joly et al.
(Creative Discoveries)
Includes index.
Summary: Describes various careers and occupations of people around the world,
including farmers, lumberjacks, and construction workers.
ISBN: 0-88682-954-2
1. Vocational guidance—Juvenile literature.   2. Occupations—Juvenile literature.   3. Professions—Juvenile literature.
[1. Occupations.]   I. Barbey, Dorine.   II. Dupas, Alain.   III. Title.   IV. Series.
HF5381.2.J6513   1999
331.7′02—dc21   First Edition   97-23938
2 4 6 8 9 7 5 3 1

PEOPLE
AT WORK

CONTENTS

CREATIVE EDUCATION

Do you dream about a job you would like to do one day? All occupations require skill and experience. People don't become butchers or architects overnight. They must learn their chosen trades before they can practice them. This may involve studying at a university, or working and learning on the job.

A press for squeezing oil out of olives

Some jobs are much older than others. For thousands of years, people have relied on farmers to work the land and raise animals for food. Other jobs don't exist yet. In 20 years, you may be doing a job that no one does today. Many trades have disappeared through the years. Some jobs are now done by machines, while our changing way of life has made others unnecessary.

Knife grinder

In the past, the countryside was even more lively. Growing crops and raising animals used to keep most of the population busy. Nearly everyone lived in the country. Not only did farmers live in the country, but so did shepherds, who tended flocks of sheep, and people who looked after geese. At harvest time, workers arrived at the farms to help farmers bring in their wheat or pick their apples or olives.

A whole range of skilled tradesmen made and repaired the farmers' tools. The wheelwright fixed the farmers' carts and wagons. The knife grinder made a living sharpening knives, scissors, and other cutting tools. Don't confuse him with the tinker, who traveled from farm to farm mending holes in pots and pans.

Some merchants made a lot of noise. In the past, people bought things from merchants who had stalls or who walked through the city streets. Many merchants let people know they had something to sell by playing music. People called hawkers wore colorful clothes and shouted at the top of their voices to amuse people, attract their attention, and make them reach for their purses. Later, merchants began to sell their goods from shops. These were often in dark, narrow city streets, so the shopkeepers had to call to passersby to get noticed. In Europe during the Middle Ages, different streets or parts of towns became well-known for different trades: people could buy cloth in Draper's Lane and bread in Baker Street. This way the merchants could keep an eye on their competitors.

A miller heads for the market with a sack of flour he has ground.

Today the range of occupations is almost endless. In offices, shops, and factories, on the sea and in the air, as well as on land, even through the night as you sleep, people go on working.

 **We depend on farmers to supply our food.** Farming is one of the oldest, most widespread jobs in the world. Farmers work the land with great care and patience. They plow, plant, weed, and harvest with the rhythm of the seasons. The animals that farmers raise provide milk and meat, and in some parts of the world, they help with the work in the fields.

"Make hay while the sun shines." In the past there weren't weather forecasts. Farmers followed age-old advice like this and watched for natural signs to help them organize their work. Using simple tools, farmers grew cereals such as wheat, from which flour for bread is made. Where the land was too steep, they built stone steps to stop the soil from being washed away. Fields had to be left to rest, or lie fallow, from time to time because farming soon depleted the soil. In summer, the busy season, farmers started work at dawn and kept going until it was too dark to work.

In many parts of the world today, people are still farming in the traditional way with animals and basic tools.

Before the autumn storms came, the wheat had to be cut, tied together in sheaves, and threshed. The grain then had to be stored in a granary. The leftover straw was used for bedding for the animals. After the crops had been harvested in autumn, farmers did other types of work during the winter. They cut wood, repaired their tools, or wove wicker baskets. If the winter was harsh or the spring was too rainy, the first harvest may not have been good enough to fill the granary.

In China, water buffalo pull a plow through rice paddies.

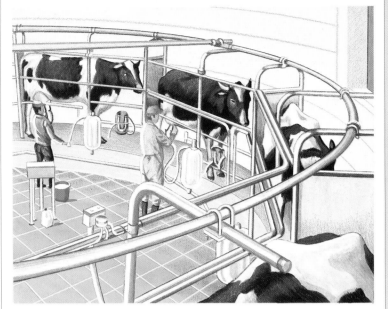

On a modern dairy farm, the cows line up and wait their turn to be milked by machine.

Today farmers grow cash crops to sell instead of keeping them to eat. They specialize in certain crops according to region. Much of the world's corn and wheat is grown on the prairies, while coffee and bananas are abundant in the Tropics. Rice is grown on marshlands.

The tractor has made farmers' jobs easier. Driving this powerful machine, farmers turn over the soil in spring and drag a harrow to break up clods of earth. If rainfall is low, powerful sprinklers water the crops they've planted. In some places, chemical fertilizers are used to enrich the soil. In late summer, a machine called the combine is used to harvest some crops.

In long buildings, chickens are raised by the thousands for the eggs they lay. When a chicken lays an egg, it is collected automatically. It drops from the chicken's pen onto a conveyor belt and is carried to a room where it is inspected and packaged for shipment to market.

A combine can harvest in hours a field that once took several days.

The veterinarian has been called out in the night to look after a sick cow.

A plow attached to a tractor saves time by digging several straight furrows for planting on each pass.

Oranges need plenty of water and sunshine to grow and ripen.

Fruit trees can be trained to grow into various shapes. Apple and pear trees are sometimes grown flat against a wall.

Grapes grow on a vine that is usually trained along wires so it can produce large bunches of good quality grapes.

Some trees and shrubs are sold with their roots protected by a ball of soil. Others are sold with their roots exposed.

Grapes are grown in vineyards. In late summer, some growers hire extra workers to pick the ripe grapes. In winter, the vines are protected with straw at their bases. But a late frost in spring may damage or kill the plants.

Apples, oranges, and pears grow in orchards. To protect trees from disease, the fruit farmer may spray them with chemicals. In winter, the farmer trims the branches and turns over the soil to cover the tree roots.

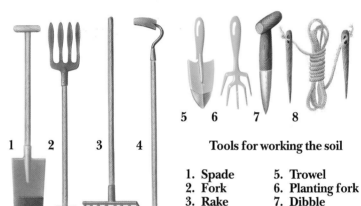

Tools for working the soil

1. Spade
2. Fork
3. Rake
4. Hoe

5. Trowel
6. Planting fork
7. Dibble
8. Garden line

The trees in our yards often come from a nursery. At the nursery, gardeners grow baby trees, called saplings, in the most favorable conditions. They make sure the young trees are in good soil and have enough heat and water. The best time to buy trees is autumn or early spring.

Have you ever heard the ear-splitting roar of chain saws near your home? Look up, and you may see a tree surgeon at work, perched high on a branch. On city streets there is not much room for trees to grow. In winter, tree surgeons prune the branches that have become too big and are getting in the way of houses or power lines. If the tree has been damaged in a storm, the tree surgeon may paint the wounds with chemicals to protect them. Correct pruning is also vital for the health of the tree. In the forest, loggers cut down trees. In the past they worked with axes and hand saws. The wood was dragged away by horses or floated downstream to the nearest sawmill.

Loggers use powerful cranes to pick up and load logs onto trucks. These trucks transport the logs to sawmills to be cut into lumber and processed into other products.

These days, lumberjacks use chain saws to trim the trees and strip them of their branches. The trees are then loaded onto timber trucks and taken to the sawmill.

Chain saw

Billhook

Protective chemical

Saw

"Timber!" Loggers must cut trees so they fall in the right direction—away from other workers in the forest. When a tree begins to fall, the logger shouts so everyone will be aware of the danger. Foresters look after trees in the forest and in the city. They plant young trees, thin out weaker trees, and check for pests and diseases. They try to grow as many healthy trees as they can.

Our cities and towns can change quickly. Where a block of houses may have stood one year, an overpass stands in the next. In our modern world, new construction is always changing the landscape. In a few months, workers can create buildings as large as those that took years, or even centuries, to build in the past.

Marble   **Sandstone**   **Limestone**

In the Middle Ages, a cathedral building site was a hive of activity. The architect was known as the master mason and was responsible for designing every part of the building: windows, vaults, ribs, and tracery. The master mason combined some of what had been done before with new ideas to design the building. That is why all cathedrals look a little bit alike and yet each is quite different. Once the master mason had drawn up the plans, foundations were dug and the stone was quarried.

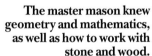

The master mason knew geometry and mathematics, as well as how to work with stone and wood.

Step by step, the master mason directed the artisans in their work. Paid by the week or by the day, the laborers usually lived in the city or nearby villages. Sculptors and masons were highly skilled artisans. They came from all over Europe and spent their lives traveling from one building site to another.

The master mason visited the quarry to select the best building material.

Carpenters balanced on beams high above the ground. They nailed together heavy wooden beams for the framework of the stone building, as well as building platforms for the workers to stand on.

Carpenters

The masons had to be very precise. They joined the stones together with mortar, a mixture of cement, lime, sand, and water. When a layer of stones had been laid, they checked with a level and plumb line to make sure it was even.

Masons

Sculptors carved and decorated the stone before it was put in place. They shaped large blocks of stone with pick-axes and chisels. Often the blocks were marked with a symbol to show where they would fit in the building according to the master mason's plans. Tools and nails for the builders were forged on site by the blacksmith. Many carpenters were kept busy building scaffolding and ladders, as well as making blocks and tackle to lift heavy stones.

Sculptors

The roofs were often covered with lead.

But things did not always go as planned. Cathedrals could take 50 to 100 years to build—or longer. Sometimes the master masons got their calculations wrong, and, after many years, part of the cathedral might collapse. It would then have to be redesigned and built up again.

Machines called windlasses were used to raise the blocks of stone as the walls grew higher.

Giant machines are used to construct modern buildings.

Whether digging a tunnel under the sea, leveling a hill, or linking an island to the mainland with a bridge, it seems as if nothing is impossible for today's builders. In the office, the architect checks the plans one last time. But at the building site, the engines have already begun to roar. The mammoth machines drill, dig, break rocks, move earth, and level the surface.

Supervisors oversee the work on a building site.

Workers use machines to prepare the soil where the foundations of the new building will be placed. Skyscrapers must be able to withstand strong winds, changes in temperature, earthquakes, and other forces of nature. They rest on foundations built down into the ground. In soft ground, piles are sunk deep to make a solid base. The foundations are covered by a concrete slab.

Cement storage

Concrete mixer

Bulldozer

Pneumatic hammer

Backhoe

Power shovel

Dump truck

Different building materials are needed for various jobs.

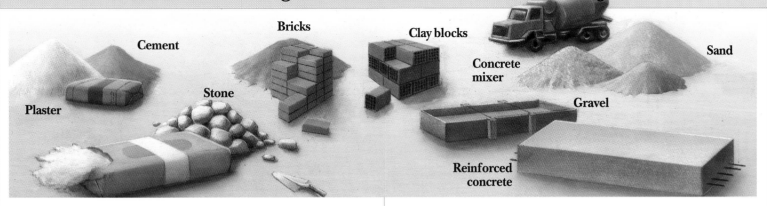

Plaster, Cement, Bricks, Stone, Clay blocks, Concrete mixer, Sand, Gravel, Reinforced concrete

What materials do we use for building?
Some traditional materials, such as brick and stone, have been used for thousands of years. Bricks are made of molded clay baked until it is hard; stone is cut from quarries. To join bricks or stones together, builders use mortar. Finished walls may be covered with a smooth plaster surface, called drywall, or many other materials.

Skyscrapers may be made of steel, reinforced concrete, or prestressed concrete. These materials have revolutionized architecture since the 1900s. Concrete is a mixture of sand, gravel, cement, and water. A mold is built in which the concrete is poured. After the concrete has hardened, the molds are removed. When reinforced with bars of steel, called rebar, running through it, concrete is very strong. In prestressed concrete, the steel bars have been stretched as much as possible before the concrete is poured. Steel girders radiating out from the skyscraper's core support the different floors. More girders make the skeleton for the outer walls.

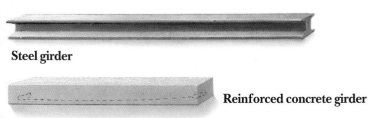

Steel girder

Reinforced concrete girder

The steel framework of a skyscraper isn't visible because it is covered by reflective glass windows. This special glass filters out the sun's harmful rays but lets in light.

Work begins long before the building is started. The owner decides what type of building to build and pays for the work. The architect draws up the plans and gives the owner's ideas shape. Civil engineers study the technical problems and decide which materials will best suit the job.

Pneumatic compactor

If all the rules and regulations for safety and the environment have been followed, the town or city council will grant permission for the new building. Cranes and other machines arrive and the construction work starts. The engineer studies any technical problems and checks the strength of the materials.

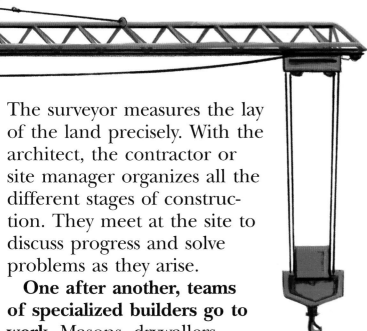

The surveyor measures the lay of the land precisely. With the architect, the contractor or site manager organizes all the different stages of construction. They meet at the site to discuss progress and solve problems as they arise.

One after another, teams of specialized builders go to work. Masons, drywallers, carpenters, window installers, plumbers, painters, electricians, and heating and cooling specialists—they all have their particular skills and take over at the right time. The drywaller follows the electrician and the plumber to plug up the holes where wires and pipes pass. And the painter doesn't wet his brushes until the carpenter is finished.

Signs are usually posted at the site, which read "Danger—Do Not Enter." People are not allowed in without wearing hard hats because the site is a dangerous place.

As the skyscraper grows higher and higher, the construction workers' jobs become more difficult. Perched on scaffolding high above the city, workers must be slow and careful when they move. Down below, on solid ground, the supervisor directs the workers' movements by talking to them on a radio. If frost or rain slows the work down, workers race against the clock to make up for lost time. The site manager has promised to finish the building by a fixed date.

When the building is nearly completed, the interior decorator pays a visit. Fixing up the inside of the building is his or her job. This may involve putting up partition walls or installing gardens with fountains in the main lobby of the building. Then furniture is chosen, and pictures are hung on the walls. The construction is nearing completion.

A concrete core supports the tower in the middle.

This building is covered with reflective glass set in aluminum frames.

Cars, clothes, refrigerators, and plastic toys are some of the many things mass-produced in factories. Based on models, each item is nearly identical to the next. Factories operate day and night. The machines are expensive and must run non-stop to pay for themselves.

In the 19th century, when the first factories were built, workers put in long hours in harsh conditions. People often spent more than 14 hours a day, 6 days a week, sweating over their machines.

Working conditions and hours have changed and improved a lot since then. Now, every eight hours, a new team of workers comes to work. The hours may vary, but a typical day at a factory might have a schedule such as this: at 8 a.m., the night shift leaves and the day shift takes over until 4 p.m. They are replaced by the evening shift workers, who work until midnight. Night shift workers have to sleep during the day.

At each stage of production, workers carry out precise tasks related to their training. Standing over their machines under the watchful eye of a supervisor, the most experienced workers might cut, adjust, or stamp pieces of metal. Further along on a conveyor belt, others might assemble or sort. They all work on an assembly line, each repeating the same task again and again. They must be quick and precise or the line will slow down.

Robots are being used more and more in the automobile industry and in factories where metal is produced.

With its jointed arm, this robot can grab very heavy objects and place them several feet away.

With their arms operated by remote control, robots can quickly load, unload, and pick up extremely hot metal objects to be plunged into cooling baths.

Machines can be quick and tireless workers.

In the early 1900s, assembly line workers put together metal sardine cans.

Many people have been afraid that machines would put them out of work. But many people now have jobs keeping an eye on the machines, servicing and repairing them when they break down. At the end of the production line, workers check the quality of the products or test the products' strength. Because of automation, people are free to do more challenging and rewarding work.

The workers have sophisticated machines, or robots, to help them in this car factory production line.

Soldering all the parts of a car's body to the chassis or painting the metal with a special gun: these tasks can be jobs for robots. In automobile factories, human workers can now avoid the most repetitive, tiring, and dangerous tasks thanks to the work of robots. Robots also save time because they never get tired.

Machine tools can work on their own, too. Like robots, machine tools are automatic; they can make a series of actions one after the other. According to the program in its memory, the machine tool pierces, engraves, flattens, or rounds all sorts of objects. Change its program and it will perform a different operation.

The increase in the use of automatic machines in factories is called automation. In the last few decades, factories have become more and more automated. This has transformed the roles of human workers. Machines now do many of the jobs once done by people on industrial assembly lines. The machines do the hard work, while humans make sure the machines keep running.

It takes years to become a skilled artisan.

From a piece of metal, a ball of wool, a piece of leather, or a block of wood, the nimble hands of a skilled artisan can shape objects that take form as if by magic. Every piece an artisan produces is handmade and unique.

Early people thought that the blacksmith had supernatural powers. The blacksmith's skilled hands created useful tools and harmful weapons in the fire.

The carpenter works wood on a bench. He uses a plane to smooth the uneven surface and to polish the wood.

At the wheelwright's workshop, workers are busy making and repairing the wheels of wagons and carts.

Long ago, artisans grouped together by trade into various guilds. Every member of a guild agreed to guard the secrets of the trade. Guilds helped set prices and maintain quality in their products.

In medieval times, the young apprentice learned a trade by working in a master's studio as an assistant. The apprentice began by doing the simplest tasks. The title of journeyman was earned by traveling and working the country for four or five years. In studios and workshops, the apprentice discovered the special styles and production techniques of different regions. After returning, the apprentice became a master by producing a masterpiece, a piece of work showing off the skills of the apprentice's trade.

The blacksmith heats iron at a forge so it will melt and can be worked and shaped with a hammer.

The crwth is a stringed instrument played long ago in Wales.

Minstrels in the Middle Ages played the rebeck.

In the countryside, artisans once lived side by side with peasants. The wheelwright repaired the farmer's wagon wheels and the blacksmith forged and fixed metal shoes for the farmer's horses.

The violin maker's tools

Most artisans were found in the city. Specializing in working metal, wood, or textiles, artisans grouped together in the same streets or districts so customers knew where to find them. Their tiny, dark homes were often above or behind their workshops. Today, mass production in factories has eliminated many crafts. Others will never disappear because they cannot be done by machines.

Antonio Stradivari (1644–1737), an Italian artisan, once made the finest violins in the world. Today the instruments he built are very valuable.

It takes an enormous amount of time, skill, and patience to make a violin. The violin maker cuts out, shapes, glues, drills, sands, assembles, and varnishes many pieces of special wood. Machines, no matter how precise, could not do the work of the violin maker's delicate hands. The sound of the finished violin depends entirely on the artisan's skill. The violin maker studies the angle and thickness of the bridge and must choose the best materials for the instrument.

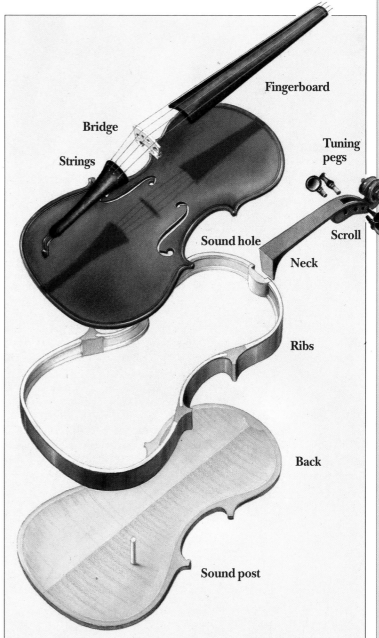

Fingerboard
Bridge
Tuning pegs
Strings
Scroll
Sound hole
Neck
Ribs
Back
Sound post

Artists need inspiration to guide their skills.

In the calm of a studio or perched high on scaffolding in a church, painters are busy working. Their movements are guided by skill and inspiration. The art they produce may inspire future generations of artists for centuries.

Standing behind an easel, the artist applies small strokes of paint to a canvas stretched across a wooden framework.

The artist mixes ground powders of pigment, or color, with oil on a palette. By combining a few primary colors in various proportions, the artist can create an infinite variety of subtle and bold shades.

The model stays still as she poses. Her expression and the position of her body must remain as natural as possible.

Sculptors create images in three dimensions.

The talents of artists are typically judged on their originality, the meaning of their works, and the harmony of the colors or shapes they create.

Medieval sculptors carved beautiful images. Look up at the top of a cathedral's columns, and you'll see carved images. In the Middle Ages, few people could read, and art had to teach as well as impress. Each carving told part of a Bible story. Large compositions were carved from stone blocks on site; smaller scenes were brought to the site from the sculptor's private workshop.

The cathedral carvings often represented the life of Christ or described Biblical events.

The calipers, mallet, drill bits, cold chisel, and hammer are the sculptor's main tools.

Sculptors work with marble, wood, and metal, as well as with stone. Under the continual blows of the hammer and chisel, details appear—folds in clothing, curls of hair, or facial expressions. The precise details and texture of a sculpture can give it a lifelike appearance.

At the top, Christ presides over the Last Judgment. At the bottom, the archangel Michael weighs a person's virtues against his or her sins.

The west door of the cathedral in Bourges, France

Stained glass windows are made from colored glass. Medieval glass makers were unable to make large panes. They laid small pieces together over a sketch, called a cartoon, made on cloth or paper. Metal oxides added to the glass while it was in liquid form produced the colors. The pieces were joined together with strips of lead, and the decorated panels were fixed into window openings.

Colored glass has been used in the windows of Christian churches since the fifth century.

Often, merchants and artisans paid for a cathedral window. In exchange, the glass makers placed small images of the donors in the stained glass window. A close look behind the Apostles or the Virgin Mary in these windows may reveal a blacksmith forging horseshoes or a baker selling bread.

Painting a stained glass window adds details and gives the figures shape and depth.

Weavers turn rolls of colored thread into cloth, tapestries, carpets, and rugs. In the past, they wove enormous tapestries to decorate the walls of churches and castles. The weaver starts by stretching rows of long threads called the warp over a frame. Then a shuttle is used to intertwine the weft and warp threads. Weft threads run perpendicular to the warp.

The glass maker's tools: a glass cutter and a pair of pliers

The weaver always works on the reverse side of the tapestry. After several passes of the shuttle, the weaver packs down the weft threads with a special comb to keep the work straight. It can take a month to produce one square yard (.836 sq m). The large and intricate tapestries seen today in museums took many years to weave.

Goldsmiths and silversmiths work gold, silver, and gilded metals like platinum and bronze to produce metal plates, trays, or candlesticks. On the surfaces of metal objects, the smiths create scenes and engrave or chisel decorations. They may also apply ornaments such as precious stones, colored glass, or pieces of enamel to the objects. With the help of tiny instruments and strong lenses, jewelers use some of the same techniques to make rings, necklaces, and brooches.

A goldsmith's or silversmith's work

Metals are enameled using one of two French methods. In champlevé, the artisan leaves hollows in the metal and fills them with liquid enamel. In cloisonné, different colors of enamel are kept apart by thin strips of metal soldered together to form little compartments.

The design for a stained glass window is traced onto a piece of canvas the same size as the window and divided into blocks of color. A piece of glass in the correct color is cut to the shape of each different colored block. Then the artisans piece them together like a jigsaw puzzle and join them with strips of lead.

The history of trade is as old as the history of civilization.

The butcher sells meat, and the baker sells bread; the grocer sells fruit and vegetables. Every time we exchange money or goods for something we want, we are trading. Merchants have always traded. We rely on merchants for the goods and services we need every day.

In the Middle Ages, the butcher sold mostly salted meat.

The grocer sells a little of everything: ham, milk, candy, sugar, fruits and vegetables, chocolate, spices, and even newspapers. In the past there were grocery stores every few blocks. In the Middle Ages there were small shopkeepers everywhere: rope makers, cobblers, and knife grinders.

Merchants, peddlers, and shopkeepers bought and sold goods.

Roman merchant

The citizens of Rome could buy almost anything they wanted. Roman merchants brought back perfumes from Arabia, wheat from Egypt, rhinoceros horn from Africa, and smoked ham from Gaul. These exotic products were sold in the markets and corner shops of Rome.

In the Middle Ages, rich shopkeepers had stalls opening onto the pavement. They displayed their wares under a canopy to protect them from the rain. At night, traders closed their shops by locking two shutters.

The apothecary made ointments and lotions and sold medicines made from plant extracts. Modern pharmacies developed from the precise work of the apothecary.

People in the Middle Ages found the barber or the draper by looking for the wrought iron signs in the shape of a shaving dish and a roll of cloth.

Merchants discussed the price of goods between themselves before selling them to shopkeepers.

A peddler was a traveling salesman. Peddlers traveled from village to village with carts full of goods, or with their backs loaded down with wares. Peddlers sold all sorts of treasures—pots and pans, cloth, brooms, and farming tools. People in remote places depended on peddlers for news as well as for their shopping. They were always glad to see peddlers coming up the road.

People of the Middle Ages could recognize traveling merchants by their cries. "Herrings, fat juicy herrings!" "Ribbons and lace!" As dawn broke, the merchants wandered around town shouting out what they had to sell. Crowds hurried into the narrow streets to buy cured meat, dried fish, salt, and other foods. There were also merchants who sold material to make clothes and cobblers who mended old boots.

The grocer

Long ago, merchants crossed the seas, mountains, and burning deserts. They set sail for the far corners of the globe to buy or sell exotic, expensive goods such as silk, spices, and precious metals.

In the 13th century, Italian merchants controlled trade with the Far East. Every year, hundreds of large sailing ships left Venice and Genoa. The merchants returned with spices and great rolls of silk. These luxuries were sold at the wharf at high prices, and paid for with gold coins called ducats.

Traveling merchants often had to pay a tax or toll before they were allowed to cross a bridge or enter a town.

For the last part of the journey to China, Arab merchants took over. They traveled by land, with large caravans of loaded camels. Thousands of camels set off from Constantinople on the long route to Asia known as the Silk Road, a trade route first used by the Roman Empire. The merchants had to overcome freezing cold, scorching heat, and thieves who lay in wait to steal the merchants' loads.

During the Middle Ages, European merchants traveled from town to town. They visited markets and fairs year round. Fairs were held over several days or even weeks. There were jugglers, fire eaters, and acrobats entertaining people in the streets while merchants sold their wares. People flocked to the fairs. In some towns, market halls were built for merchants to store their goods. They could also sleep there and have their money changed into different currencies.

A cruel trade developed between Africa and the New World. African men, women, and children were captured and sent to work as slaves on plantations in North America and the West Indies. They were bought and sold like goods. The conditions on slave ships were so bad that many thousands died during the trip.

Slaves for sale at a market

All these goods were brought to Europe from the New World. Today we take it for granted that we can buy them in our grocery stores.

Merchants sailed the world in search of rare goods and new luxuries. Spanish galleons rushed to the New World and returned in slow convoys loaded with gold and silver. If they were lucky, they managed to escape the Caribbean pirates and the terrible storms of the Atlantic!

In the 16th and 17th centuries, the seaport cities of Europe grew rich on trade. Gold from Brazil, spices and tea from India and Ceylon, sugar from the West Indies, and porcelain from China were brought to Seville, Nantes, Amsterdam, and London.

It could take two or three years for a Dutch cargo ship to make the journey to the West Indies and return with its valuable cargo. The holds of these ships were packed with diamonds, porcelain, and spices which made fortunes for the merchants in Antwerp and Amsterdam.

Europe's empires were based on trade. The nations of Europe fought for new colonies and the riches they contained.

After Holland, Britain became the largest trading power. Fast clipper ships brought tea from China and India to London.

Outside of large cities, thousands of people work hard to produce the food we buy at the grocery store. Dairy farms produce milk. Large feedlots raise cattle and hogs that are shipped to slaughter houses for processing. Fishing boats travel far out to sea to provide fresh seafood, and farms grow fruits and vegetables to be sold as fresh produce at our local markets. Refrigerated trucks are used to transport the food and keep it fresh.

Even in the middle of winter we can enjoy oranges, tomatoes, bananas, and strawberries. These fruits are grown in Florida, California, and Central America. Fruit, vegetables, meat, fish, and cheese can be transported quickly over long distances.

People may choose many different ways of buying and selling goods today. We can order items by telephone or through the mail, pay for our selections with a credit card or check, and have goods delivered to our door. We can shop day or night on the Internet.

Some things still can be purchased from street vendors while others can be purchased at home on the computer.

. . . but all over the world, people go shopping at markets.

A Chinese supermarket on the island of Taiwan

In North African markets called souks, business is conducted in the open air.

Markets are still the most widespread system of trading. In Africa, Asia, and South America, people often travel long distances to sell their own vegetables and poultry. They arrive at their stalls early in the morning and spread out their fruits or vegetables on mats of straw or bright cloth. In North Africa, each town has a covered market called a souk where artisans make and sell their goods. At the back of a stall, a carpet-seller might talk to a customer over a glass of mint tea. The sale may take hours while they haggle over the price, which is never fixed in advance.

In the crowded streets of these Arab cities, walking salespeople watch for possible customers. Some salespeople are still children. Just like merchants everywhere, business people at the souk buy in bulk and sell small amounts for a profit.

It is common to see floating markets in Bangkok, Thailand. Little boats loaded with watermelons, coconuts, papayas, or pineapples arrive early in the morning. People go from boat to boat comparing prices before buying what they want.

People receive letters from Australia, eat oranges from California, and play with electronic games made in Japan. How do all these things get to us? Sailors, drivers, and pilots carry letters, goods for trade, and travelers by the millions every day. These people work in the field of transportation.

Roman messengers once carried orders and letters from one side of the empire to the other on well-constructed roads. About every 10 miles (16 km) they found rest stops where they exchanged their exhausted horses for fresh ones. These messengers covered as much as 40 miles (64 km) in a day. Across the Roman Empire, nearly 50,000 miles (80,000 km) of roads were built. Shiploads of merchandise passed through the great Mediterranean ports. Barcelona, Naples, Venice, Marseilles, Athens, and Tangiers have all known busy traffic since ancient times.

Salt was packed in barrels and often transported by river in the Middle Ages.

Journeys by chariot or on horseback were very slow. Merchants preferred to take advantage of natural waterways where goods could be transported on boats or rafts. Sometimes they built artificial waterways called canals. Sailors used horses to tow barges, following towpaths along the canals. To get through tunnels, the sailors lay on their backs and pushed the walls with their feet. Cities on rivers became ports and centers of trade.

In the 1860s, a stagecoach trip from Missouri to California could take 25 days or more.

The stagecoach driver was the king of the road in the 18th century. The driver needed great skill to maneuver the coach across rough terrain in order to arrive at the next stop in one piece. The stage-coach stopped every few miles. An inn-keeper provided food and drink for the driver and his passengers and supplied fresh horses for the stagecoach.

Two hundred years ago, many people crossed the city in an omnibus, a long, horse-drawn carriage. There were often two classes of passengers. The cheapest seats were on the roof, exposed to the wind and rain. Passengers climbed an iron ladder mounted on the outside. There were no set stops; the driver stopped when someone hailed him. Later, a motor was used in place of the team of horses, and the bus was born.

Delivery people used horse-drawn wagons to transport sacks of coal, ice, and bread. The whole city smelled of horses.

On foot, dragging heavy wheelbarrows, water carriers delivered water for hot baths to the homes of people who could afford it. The carriers lugged large containers of hot water up many flights of narrow stairs. No one had running water, so many people used water from springs, rivers, and public fountains.

A funicular, or cable railway, can climb steep mountains.

Sitting at the controls of a high-speed express, the train engineer races across the country-side. With eyes glued to the command panel, the engineer doesn't have time to admire the landscape as it rushes by. Today the trains are guided by computers that pass on the necessary signals to the engineer. At any moment, the engineer can check the brakes and motor on a computer screen or take over in case of an emergency. These security precautions are essential because rail traffic has become so heavy, especially in Europe. Day and night around the world, trains transport millions of passengers and thousands of tons of merchandise. In the United States, cross-country train use has declined, but new, high-speed trains are used by commuters in big cities.

Truck stops stay open 24 hours a day to provide services and goods for trucks and truck drivers.

Truck drivers spend many hours in the driver's seat in order to transport the merchandise and raw materials people and businesses need. In the United States, trucks transport more freight than trains. To find out about traffic problems, and also just for fun, truck drivers talk to each other on CB radios. Of course, they have to stay alert because driving is a risky business, and their trucks are often loaded with dangerous substances such as gasoline and other chemicals.

Some high speed trains can carry people at speeds of 150 miles (240 km) per hour.

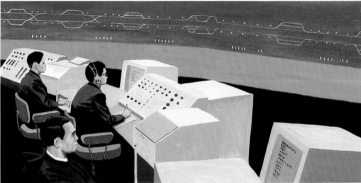

To avoid accidents, railroad tracks are controlled by signalers. Engineers watch for colored signal lights along the track.

Going in and out of stations, trains are guided by a system of points. These are regulated electronically from a signal box.

"Prepare for take-off!" the captain announces. Airplanes can cover longer distances than any other modern form of transport. Aircraft can whisk you to far-away continents, or even around the world, in a matter of hours. Freight is carried in cargo planes specially designed and built to fly with large loads. A hundred years ago, flying was still a dream. But since the first flight by the Wright Brothers in 1903, our skies have become even more crowded with planes. Airplanes carry almost 750 million passengers every year. Tracked from the ground by radio and radar, they are capable of flying at night as well as during the day. Before departure, pilots prepare a flight plan, choosing the best route according to the weather and the altitude of the flight.

In the airport tower, air traffic controllers watch the planes on radar and guide them on their takeoffs and landings.

Today, it takes only 10 sailors to run the largest ocean-going vessel. Thanks to satellites, sailors can calculate their position on the ocean with pinpoint precision. Radar allows them to locate obstacles at night or in fog. Modern ships are equipped with sonar, allowing them to calculate the depth of the water. Even the sailor at the ship's wheel has help from an automatic pilot.

Pilots of large planes must follow air corridors when they fly. These designated paths in the sky keep airplanes from colliding.

Protecting, guarding, and helping others

Day and night, men and women are keeping watch on the street, in sports stadiums, in public parks, and in stores. They are there to prevent accidents and robberies, ready to help people in trouble at any moment. The people who defend our security may work for the city or state, like police officers, or for the federal government, like soldiers. Others are hired by private companies as security guards in office buildings or factories.

Firefighters

At a museum, there may be a man or a woman in every room keeping an eye on the valuable collections. These security guards are hired to give visitors directions or to stop them from touching or stealing the paintings they are admiring. These guards also work at night, making the rounds and checking the electronic alarm system.

In movie theaters, shopping malls, or airports, the security guards are not always visible. But they are behind the scenes, watching out for thieves, checking the emergency doors, and keeping customers safe. Many buildings are now monitored by hidden video cameras, and the guards are in constant contact with the local police and fire departments.

Twenty-four hours a day in every neighborhood, police officers are on the beat. They pass by in their patrol cars, keeping the streets safe for all citizens. In the safety of their houses, people know that the police are there to guard them from prowlers. When a call comes over the radio, the police officers turn on the patrol car's lights and siren and rush off to the scene of the crime to catch the thieves. Police stations are open all night trying to solve crimes. Police officers work hard and sometimes risk their lives to keep our neighborhoods safe.

Firefighters risk their lives to help others.

Early 17th century hand pump

Used in France, this long ladder can go up to 100 feet (30 m) high and turn around. Beside the fire truck is an ambulance.

One of the biggest dangers of all is fire. The first firefighters were Roman slaves. These slaves patrolled the cities, putting out any fires that had started.

In the Middle Ages, most people lived in wooden houses that went up in flames very quickly. The blazes spread fast through the narrow streets. The watchman was responsible for giving the alarm when fires started. Then the people of the city set up human chains to fetch and deliver water in buckets from the river or a well. Carpenters tore down the parts of the houses in the grip of the fire. This often sapped the fire's strength, making it easier to put out.

An early Dutch water squirt

The first fire engines were built in the 17th century. They were hand pumps mounted on sleds or wheels, and could be pulled to the raging fire.

Later, when carts began being pulled by horses, help arrived more quickly. Gasoline-powered fire engines were first built at the beginning of the 20th century. The engine drove the vehicle to the fire and then powered the pump.

Fire has caused some terrible disasters. The Chicago Fire of 1871 destroyed 3.5 square miles (9 sq km) of the city and killed 250 people. Sparks from the fire started forest fires in Michigan and Wisconsin.

This early 20th century fire engine could get to the fire fast, pulling a heavy load.

The forest fires lasted six days and destroyed over one million acres (405,000 ha) of timberland. The fires killed more than 1,000 people. It was the worst fire tragedy in American history.

Firefighters are highly trained.

At the fire station, the alarm rings out its warning. When a fire is reported, the dispatcher calls the fire station and the firefighters rush to get ready, leaving whatever they were doing. They slide down the pole that gets them from their sleeping quarters to the garage in the quickest time possible. The fire engines in the garage are always filled with water and ready to go. In less than a minute, the firefighters are on the fire engine and on their way to the fire. Out on the streets and highways, other drivers must get out of the way so the firefighters can get through.

While training to carry the injured, one firefighter pretends to be hurt.

Firefighters have to be physically fit. They train many hours a week so that they can react instantly in an emergency and know exactly what to do. There is a tower at the fire station where they practice rescuing people or using their hoses while standing on a ladder. They learn first aid. During training, they are sent into rooms filled with smoke so they will learn how to work in smoke-filled buildings without being able to see.

Firefighters must move faster than the fire if they are to beat it. The fire chief gives his orders over the two-way radio. He tells the firefighters exactly where to aim their hoses and calls for more help when it's needed. Some hoses are remote controlled; they reach into places too hot and dangerous for firefighters to go.

White smoke is a good sign. It means the firefighters are getting the fire under control.

Firefighters exercise to keep in good physical condition.

Firefighters are well equipped. They wear protective clothing to keep from being burned or injured. A helmet protects the firefighter's head and neck. When they respond to a fire, firefighters wear special clothes called turnouts to keep them cool. These are sometimes a shiny silver to reflect the heat away. When firefighters enter burning buildings, they must wear masks with air tanks because the oxygen in the room may be filled with toxic fumes. Firefighters also carry spanner wrenches to connect pieces of hose together and flashlights to help them see in dark buildings.

In communities built on waterways, some fires can only be reached with special fire boats that pump water straight from a river or the sea.

In Venice, firefighters go almost everywhere by boat.

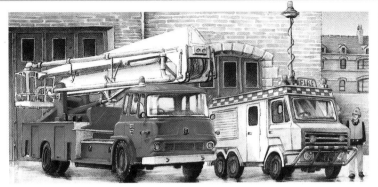

This English fire engine has a hydraulic arm.

This German amphibious vehicle is as effective on land as in the water.

In the U.S., firefighters can go high on this platform.

This Russian fire engine carries large quantities of water.

This high-speed American fire engine patrols the airport runway.

Fighting flood waters, earthquakes, and pollution . . .

Whether it's putting out a forest fire, tackling a skyscraper in flames, or battling a blaze on an oil rig at sea, firefighters deal with all sorts of disasters.

To reach the top story of a skyscraper, a special platform is suspended from a helicopter.

In summer, lightning starts most forest fires. To stop these fires from spreading, firefighters cut and dig fire breaks through the trees and soil. Helicopters and special planes drop loads of water and fire retardant onto the blaze.

Firefighters do more than put out fires.
They are often called to help when a car accident or other medical emergency occurs. They answer all sorts of other emergency calls, too. Often they are asked to help with floods. They may have to rescue flood victims stranded in houses or bring food supplies to people and animals trapped by rising water. They also come to the rescue during major disasters, such as earthquakes. When a mine caves in, or an avalanche or tornado occurs, firefighters go to work. Their specially trained dogs help find people trapped under snow or collapsed buildings.

Firefighters are called to help stop pollution.
They put inflatable barriers across water to stop an oil spill from spreading, or help keep the public safe when other hazardous materials are spilled.

Journalists bring us news from around the world.

It once took a long time for news to travel. In the past, most news was carried by word of mouth from one person to another. Today, however, millions of people buy newspapers. Their columns are full of the latest news stories, photos, and advertisements. Every day and always on time, newspapers keep us informed.

Journalists around the world interview people and travel to places where news occurs. Back in the office, news pours in by phone, fax, and Internet. Foreign correspondents fax updates on wars or elections, and local reporters call in with the latest football or lottery results. Journalists sift through all this information before they write the day's stories.

Journalists and photographers work hard to get an interview.

In the meeting room, journalists gather around the editor-in-chief. He or she decides what news is really important and which stories should go on tomorrow's front page. They must know what is most important to their readers.

Pictures, diagrams, and maps are created on a computer with a graphics palette.

On the computer, the designers fit the pictures and text together. Assistant editors write headlines and check for mistakes in grammar and spelling. Sometimes a news story breaks just before the paper goes to press. When this happens, everyone must rush to get the new story ready for the next issue.

The designer chooses pictures by looking at slides on a light table.

Newspapers go from the printer to the newsstand in a few hours.

At the printer, technicians feed a large roll of paper through the press. The metal plates that correspond to each page of the newspaper are installed in the press and inked up. As the press rolls, the plates press down onto the paper and print the text and pictures.

A modern printing press can turn out 70,000 newspapers an hour.

Once the pages are printed, they are cut and folded on other machines. The various sections are put together then to form whole newspapers, which come rolling out on conveyor belts. A technician checks copies at random to make sure that all the pages are well printed and in the right order. The newspapers are now ready to be delivered to the public.

Bundles of newspapers are delivered to the newsstands.

How do the papers reach the newsstand? In the huge loading bay, delivery people fill their trucks with bundles of papers that have been counted, tied, and labeled. By dawn, the papers arrive in neighborhoods and at newsstands around the area.

How is a television program brought to your home?

It is 6 P.M. The television news begins. The anchor person's face appears on the screen in close-up. He or she welcomes the thousands or millions of viewers who watch the live broadcast. Facing the cameras, the anchor person reports the day's events.

During a broadcast, we never see the crowd of technicians who work behind the scenes at the television station.

On the studio floor, the crew is busy at work. The camera operators are in position behind their cameras. The sound engineers check the placement of the microphones, and the lighting technicians adjust the spotlights.

The producer is responsible for organizing the program. The director decides the best way to turn the script into the pictures we will see at home. In the studio control room, the director keeps an eye on the pictures coming from each camera. Up in the gallery, the producer, director, production assistant, and technical manager make sure that everything happens as planned. In front of them, monitor screens show what each camera is shooting. The director tells the camera operators, through a microphone, whether to track in or out, or to zoom in for a close up. The technical director watches the monitors and switches from one picture to another according to the director's requirements.

Some programs are made outside the studio. The crew must go "on location" to make outside broadcasts on fires, floods, sports competitions, and political events. Whenever news happens, the crew must be ready to report it. The crew has to take cameras and lights with them. They use a mobile studio to produce the program. A sound control room, vision control room, and production gallery are squeezed inside their van full of necessary equipment.

To get close to the action and get different angles of play, cameras are positioned all around sports stadiums.

Television signals reach our homes in different ways. Television transmitters on tall towers can send signals through the air from the station to television antennas on top of our houses. The signal then travels from the antenna to the television set. This was once the only way for television to reach our homes. But now signals can also be delivered by copper cable. Or a satellite dish can be used to send the signal out into space, where it is reflected back to Earth by a satellite. At home, the signal is received by another dish and sent to the television.

In the control room, the director and the technical director supervise the show's progress.

A mobile studio

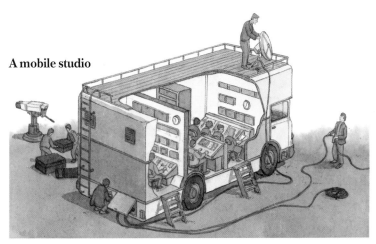

It takes a large crew of skilled people to make a movie.

Actors and actresses must audition for parts in the film.

A screenwriter creates the script.

Movies made for the theater are different from television programs. Instead of being transmitted to the television screen, movies are recorded onto photographic film. Light is then projected through the developed film onto a big screen at the theater.

To make a movie, it takes ideas, money, a lot of time, and hundreds of highly skilled workers. Under the supervision of the director, the film crew works together to create a story that will entertain, and maybe even teach, a large audience.

The screenwriter imagines and writes a screenplay, or script. He or she proposes the script to a producer, who is responsible for finding the money to make the movie. The producer must find people who are prepared to invest their money in what they think is a good idea for a film. It is always risky. The producer usually chooses the director, who decides

The art director is responsible for designing the scenery.

how to make the written script into a story told in pictures. Actors are chosen by the casting director to play the parts of the characters. Once the filming begins, the director guides the actors so they give the performance he wants.

"Scene 1, Take 1. Action!" The filming has begun.

The director oversees each shot in the movie.

The crew works hard to make the movie.

The continuity person must make sure all parts of the scene match each other.

The film crew is ready to shoot. Today they're shooting a battle scene aboard a pirate ship built inside the studio. The chief camera operator sets up the angle of the first shot. The lighting crew checks the lamps and spotlights. Sound engineers check the microphones for sound levels. The director sits in his chair, giving the final instructions.

The clapboard

"Everyone ready?" the director shouts. **"Quiet on the set. Action!"** The beginning of each scene is marked with a clapboard. Some scenes are shot again and again until the director is satisfied; each try is called a "take."

All the scenes shot in the same place are shot at the same time, even if they come in a different order in the story.

1. Some of the world's biggest and most prestigious film studios are in Hollywood, California.

2. The carpenters are busy building a ship.

3. The make-up artist is working with one of the actors, while the wardrobe artist checks the fit of a costume.

4. The properties, or "props," person collected all the items that the actors will need in the film: swords, guns, and a wooden chest.

5. The pirate ship gets its last coat of paint.

6. One of the stars practices his lines before shooting begins.

In other studios, special effects and sound experts are hard at work. With the help of visual tricks and prerecorded noises, they record scenes that would be hard to film in a natural setting. How do you make snow in a studio in summer? Wind machines blow tiny bits of polystyrene foam onto the set. What about rain? Sprayers can provide a drizzle or a downpour, whatever the script calls for. Smoke, fog, and steam are all created by machines.

The assistant editor numbers the takes and hangs them on a rack over a bin.

Fires and explosions are the jobs of experts called pyrotechnicians. They may have only one chance to blow up a building, so they must get it right. Sound effects people can provide any sort of noise the director needs: galloping horses, creaking wagon wheels, a door slamming, or the crack of a whip.

The pieces of film are joined on a splicing machine.

After the shooting, the editing begins.
The different parts of the film are put in proper order and the best takes are chosen from the many that have been shot. The editing is as important as the shooting, and the editor works side by side with the director. The soundtrack of voices and noises has to be edited, too, so that sounds and pictures match. If this is not done carefully, we might see actors' lips move before we hear what they say. The sound engineer puts on the background music and sound effects. This is called dubbing. Sometimes the film is transferred to videotape and edited electronically. The editor watches it on a video screen, selects the pictures he wants, and puts them in order. When the director is happy with the final "cut," the film negative is edited carefully to match the final version of the videotape.

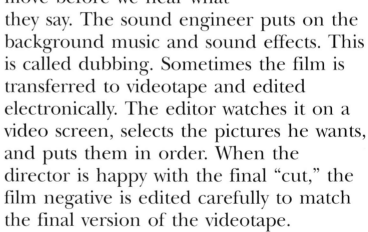

To make the wagon look as if it is being driven, the props people shake the platform it stands on while a picture of moving countryside is projected on a screen behind the action.

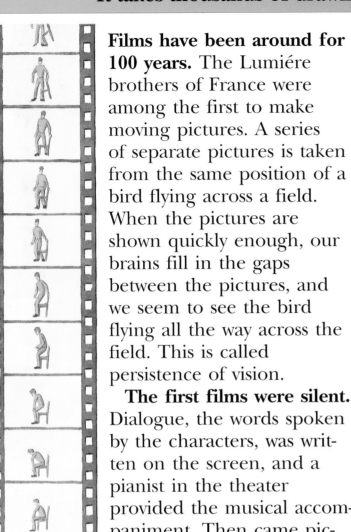

Films have been around for 100 years. The Lumiére brothers of France were among the first to make moving pictures. A series of separate pictures is taken from the same position of a bird flying across a field. When the pictures are shown quickly enough, our brains fill in the gaps between the pictures, and we seem to see the bird flying all the way across the field. This is called persistence of vision.

The first films were silent. Dialogue, the words spoken by the characters, was written on the screen, and a pianist in the theater provided the musical accompaniment. Then came pictures with sound. In 1925, the Warner Brothers introduced a sound recording system called Vitaphone. The "talkies" had arrived. Some of the great stars of silent movies never made it into talkies because their voices weren't good enough.

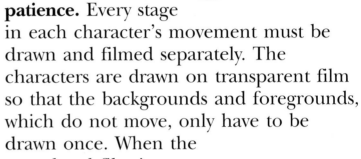

Figures and background are painted separately, then laid one on top of the other.

Making a cartoon takes a lot of patience. Every stage in each character's movement must be drawn and filmed separately. The characters are drawn on transparent film so that the backgrounds and foregrounds, which do not move, only have to be drawn once. When the completed film is projected, the character's actions seem continuous. This is another example of persistence of vision.

The Disney company became the biggest maker of animated films in the world.

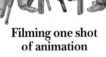

Filming one shot of animation

Today, some cartoons are made with computers. They are programmed to remember the drawings for a repeated action and can repeat them as necessary.

Actors and actresses work in the world of imagination.

If you can laugh or cry at will and like dressing up, or if you like to mimic voices and make people laugh, you may have a future as an actor or actress.

Every evening, when the curtain rises, actors and actresses come on stage. Wearing costumes and makeup, they play imaginary characters in front of an audience and give the illusion that they are real; that's the magic of theater. The performers have rehearsed the play over and over again, while the director supervises their work. They have learned their lines by heart and have practiced their voices and gestures. The performers might suffer from stage fright every evening before going on. But when the curtain rises, their fear usually disappears.

A scene from William Shakespeare's *King Lear*

Not all the action is onstage. Backstage, the stage manager is working the lights. As one scene ends, stage hands pull the set into the wings and arrange another one onstage. When a costume rips, wardrobe hands sew it. If a performer forgets a line on stage, the prompter whispers it from behind a curtain.

When the performance is over, the people cheer. The performers and stage hands will be back again the next evening for another performance.

Inside the theater: the ticket office and coat room, the balconies and boxes of seats, the stage, the backstage areas where the stage hands work, and the actors' and actresses' dressing rooms

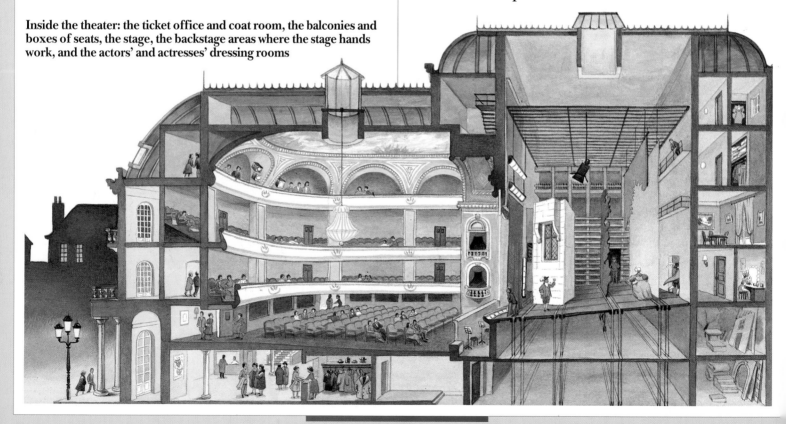

Circus artists are traveling performers.

Circus artists move from town to town or from country to country. They head for the city park, fairgrounds, or other open areas to set up their big tents. Sometimes they perform indoors in large arenas.

Underneath the Big Top, everything is music and lights. Trapeze artists swing high above the audience, with a safety net below. They must rehearse their act hundreds of times before they are ready to perform. Acrobats and animal trainers show off their skills in the ring below. The tension builds as the sword swallower and the fire-eater enter. The juggler tosses balls or burning torches into the air and catches them again with ease. Then come the clowns, tumbling around to the delight of the crowd. If the trapeze artist misses a swing or the juggler drops a ball, a clown runs in and helps them out, pretending the accident is part of the act.

A clown puts on his makeup before going into the ring.

In the cold light of dawn, the circus hands take down the Big Top and stack everything onto trucks while the tired performers sleep. In a few hours, the circus will move on to the next town.

Each musician has a place in the orchestra.

In all parts of the world, people make music. The three large families of musical instruments are percussion, such as drums; strings, such as violins; and wind, such as clarinets. The earliest musicians played percussion instruments. They used their drums to pound out a steady beat. Today they are often used for the same purpose, to help an orchestra or band maintain a rhythm.

Woodwind and brass are the two kinds of wind instruments. One of the most well-known stringed instruments is the violin.

Many different instruments playing together make up the symphony orchestra. The conductor waves his or her arms to maintain the correct tempo and to lead the musicians through the musical composition, or score. The instruments may be played separately in solos or all together.

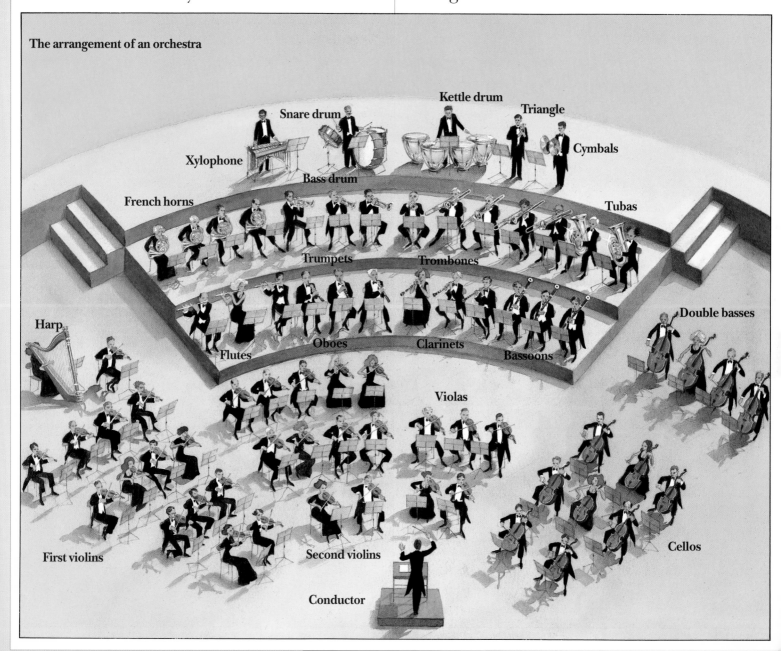

The arrangement of an orchestra

Xylophone · Snare drum · Kettle drum · Triangle · Cymbals · Bass drum · French horns · Tubas · Trumpets · Trombones · Harp · Flutes · Oboes · Clarinets · Bassoons · Double basses · Violas · First violins · Second violins · Cellos · Conductor

Jazz, blues, and rock and roll music

Jazz music was born in the southern United States from African American work songs. Jazz bands are often made up of horns, pianos, drums, and double basses. Jazz is sometimes not written down; instead the musicians start with a basic tune and make up their music as the tune develops. This is called improvisation.

The blues is a type of jazz music with a slower tempo. Blues bands often include a singer. Billie Holiday is one of the most popular blues singers of all time. A combination of blues and jazz is called rhythm and blues.

The electric guitar is one of the most common rock instruments.

Rock and roll music developed mainly from rhythm and blues. Its distinctive rhythm is usually created with drums and electric guitars. But many bands also have horn sections, pianos or other keyboards, and electronic synthesizers.

Rock and roll is an enormous industry that employs thousands of people around the world. Rock musicians do much of their work in the studio where they record their music. Once the recording is finished, they may go on tour, giving concerts in large arenas all over the world.

Doctors and nurses try to find out why you are ill . . .

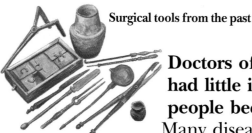
Surgical tools from the past

Doctors of the past had little idea why people became ill. Many diseases were thought to be caused by "bad blood," which was treated by bleeding the patient with the help of leeches. Early surgery was performed without anesthetics. In the Middle Ages dentists were called "denta-tores" and filled cavities with ground bone.

Hospitals are always open to help the sick and injured.

The science of medicine has made great progress in recent decades. Many of the worst illnesses have been conquered. Specialized doctors know more and more about disease and the specific functions of the human body.

The ophthalmologist is a specialist who treats diseases and other problems of vision. When we were little, most of us were probably treated by a pediatrician, who specializes in the growth and development of children. When we have problems with our skin, we see the dermatologist for treatment.

Day or night, ambulances rush to help people in need.

Doctors spend many years at medical school before they can work, or "practice medicine." Several doctors often practice together at a clinic. A medical secretary answers the phone and takes appoint-ments. Nurses take blood samples and give injections. Today, most children receive routine injections to immunize them against dangerous illnesses.

The doctor and the nurse meet an expecting mother. They will look after her and make sure all goes well.

The baby was born in the early hours of the morning. The mother has worked hard all night; now she and the father can rest.

Accidents happen at all hours of the day and night.

Emergencies require doctors and nurses to be available for their patients 24 hours a day, 7 days a week.

A little boy cries out in pain and twists and turns in his bed. His worried parents call an ambulance and the boy is rushed to the hospital emergency room. He is examined by a doctor who determines that the boy has appendicitis and must have an immediate operation.

In the operating room, the team is ready. They all wear masks and latex gloves to avoid spreading germs. The anesthesiologist gives the boy an injection to make him sleep. The surgeon, surrounded by nurses, begins the operation. "Scalpel," the surgeon says. "Scalpel," a nurse repeats, handing the surgeon a sterilized knife. After the operation, the boy will have to rest for several days while he recovers. Doctors and nurses follow his progress in the hospital and later at home.

A pharmacist's job is important, too.

Pharmacists were once called apothecaries. Apothecaries prepared their own lotions, lozenges, syrups, and ointments by grinding up and mixing plant extracts and essential oils. They used a mortar and pestle to grind their medicines. This tool is still the symbol of the pharmacist's trade. Today pharmacists mostly sell drugs developed in industrial laboratories. Some drugs, such as aspirin, are made with chemicals, while others come from plants.

A good education is a lesson for life.

Before we begin to work for our living, we need to get a good education. The idea of free public school for all children is a recent one. In past centuries, school was very expensive, and only the rich could afford to educate their children. Wealthy families hired private tutors. Most children from poor families were put to work in the fields or factories at an early age. Many were illiterate, meaning that they never learned to read or write. Now, in industrialized countries like the United States and Canada, children have the right to receive an education. Even the smallest towns now have free public grade schools and high schools.

Schools were once run with strict rules. "Do unto others as you would have them do unto you." Schoolchildren were required to memorize proverbs. Rules were strict, and if they were broken, students could be harshly punished. The school master or mistress was an important figure in the town, as respected as the local mayor.

Children may no longer walk long distances to school like their grandparents did, but they still learn how to read, write, and count in much the same way. Their teachers may now take them to visit museums and art galleries. In winter, they may go on field trips in the snow, and in summer they may take nature trips to the woods or the seaside. Students often look forward to gym class, when the teacher organizes foot races or basketball games in the school gymnasium. Many of these opportunities were not available to children a hundred years ago.

The school superintendent makes a speech at the graduation ceremony. He is wearing traditional dress for the big occasion.

Computers, tape recorders, TVs, and videos help teachers in their work. Many schools now have computers and other forms of technology in their classrooms to help students with their studies. Students might watch a video on life in Guatemala or practice their Spanish lessons by listening to a cassette. The librarian may use a computer to help students find books for class projects or good stories to read before bed. Teachers use this technology to help them pass on their knowledge.

The architecture of this school is very modern.

Many schools now have well-equipped gymnasiums and swimming pools for the students to use.

Field trips are an important part of education.

Research scientists work at the frontiers of knowledge.

Archimedes, an ancient scientist, must have been very excited when he discovered one of the mathematical principles in a sudden flash of inspiration. Research requires a lot of patience. Researchers used to lock themselves in their laboratories, lost in endless calculations. Modern scientists spend years developing and repeating experiments, slowly expanding the frontiers of knowledge. Their work may help us all live healthier, happier lives.

Today researchers work in teams specializing in areas of genetics, physics, chemistry, medicine, or agriculture. Working in small groups, the researchers divide up all the tasks to be completed.

In 1957, Russian scientists sent Sputnik, the first artificial satellite, into space.

Some teams do nothing but analyze the results. Scientists exchange ideas, explain the logic of their experiments, and even question the aims of the research. Sometimes, if their ideas didn't work, they must start over.

Technical advances pave the way for important new discoveries. In observatories, astronomers use telescopes with enormous lenses to watch the sky. They study the position and movement of stars, and sometimes discover new ones. Computers can analyze the astronomers' results, or occasionally even conduct the experiments with human guidance.

Volcanologists study the sulfurous gases that escape through gaps in the rock called fumaroles.

Scientists measure the temperature of volcanic gases.

Researchers work to make our lives better. Some try to understand how diseases are transmitted and infect the body, so that a cure can be developed. Others experiment with new medicines to make them more efficient or to get rid of their side effects. In industrial laboratories, researchers are developing light bulbs  and batteries that can last longer, planes that can carry more passengers, or cars that use less energy and cause less pollution.

Volcanologists wear masks with filters to protect their lungs from poisonous gases.

Using precise instruments, vulcanologists attempt to predict the next eruption of active volcanoes by monitoring escaping gases, vibrations of the earth, or sudden temperature changes of the volcano.

The scientist observes how a volcano is growing by measuring it from a distance.

If the volcano erupts, vulcanologists may venture onto the slopes to take samples of red hot lava. To protect their bodies from the intense heat, they wear shiny aluminum suits.

5. 4. 3. 2. 1. Lift off! Right now, several men and women are probably traveling and working in space. In 50 to 100 years, future generations may catch a space shuttle the way we catch a plane today.

Few people are chosen to journey into space. Astronauts must be strong mentally and physically. They must also be excellent pilots and scientists.

Space is a hostile environment for life. Astronauts spend years preparing to face it.

Underwater, dressed in their cumbersome space suits, astronauts exercise with the help of professional divers. They do this to get used to the weightlessness of space.

Astronauts must prepare to live for months on end cooped up in a tiny cabin. Being placed in similar conditions on Earth will help them accomplish this.

To prepare for the incredible acceleration when the rocket takes off, the astronauts are placed in a centrifuge, a machine that spins at extremely high speeds.

In the Russian space station, Mir, astronauts and cosmonauts lived and worked for periods ranging from six months to a year. In the 21st century, there may be hundreds or even thousands of people living in space stations orbiting the Earth. By then, the moon could become a scientific observatory and the first astronauts may have landed on Mars. Will you be ready for a voyage to the stars?

Velentina Tereshkova and Yuri Gagarin: the first woman and man in space

Space stations are both living quarters and workshops. They are locked in orbit around the Earth.

When completed, the International Space Station will have enough room to house seven astronauts.

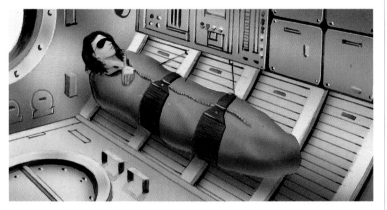

No gravity exists within the space ship. Crew members are tied to the walls to sleep.

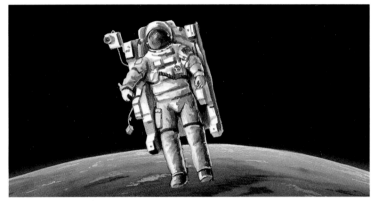

To work outside the space station, astronauts climb into space suits equipped with tiny rocket engines to help them maneuver.

The astronauts eat ready prepared meals. All they have to do is add water and reheat the food on special tables.

Astronauts use special tools to assemble the space station.

Space shuttle pilots approach the International Space Station. Sixteen nations are involved in this project.

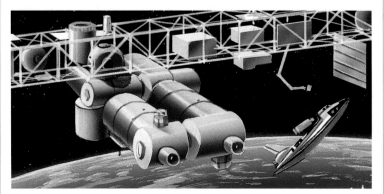

The International Space Station will be in orbit 220 miles (350 km) above the Earth.

Games and activities, a quiz, intriguing facts, a glossary, and addresses of places to visit, followed by the index

■ Did you know?

Green jobs for a greener world
New jobs are being created to help protect our environment from pollution and mismanagement.

Noise laws keep noise pollution in the city to a minimum. When a new highway is built, contractors may need to add a sound wall where the road passes close to people's houses.

Environmentalists are concerned with the health of the environment. They try to stop companies from abusing the environment by creating public pressure to get them to clean up their activities. They also try to educate the public about the dangers of pollution, hoping that people will take action.

The job game: can you guess who does what?

Without saying a word, mime the gestures of a worker and see if your friends can guess the worker's job. If it's too hard, you can help them out by giving them the first letter of the job. You can also use props, with your parents' permission, to show what a worker does.

The shuttle passes between the weaver's stretched threads.

Every job requires its own tool or instrument.
The mason: a trowel
The hairstylist: a comb, a pair of scissors
The schoolteacher: a blackboard and chalk
The butcher: an apron, a cleaver
The grocer: a set of scales
The logger: a chain saw
The pianist: a piano
The orchestra conductor: a baton
The sculptor: a hammer and chisel
The journalist or reporter: a microphone, a notepad
The lighting technician: a spotlight
The doctor: a stethoscope
The astronaut: a spacesuit
The construction worker: a hard hat
The firefighter: a helmet, an ax
The carpenter: a hammer
The painter: a paint brush

Sprucing up the appearance of a city

Landscape gardeners
study and manage parks, gardens, and sports arenas. Landscape gardeners are architects for green spaces.

In national parks or nature reserves

Foresters and biologists keep an inventory of all the plants and animals in the park and protect species that are in danger of extinction. Park rangers welcome tourists and hikers and look after public paths and campsites. They protect visitors from curious animals and protect animals from people.

In wildlife sanctuaries

Veterinary surgeons look after injured animals. Their aim is to return the wild animals to their natural habitats.

Working with animals

Zookeepers feed the animals and make sure they stay in good health.

Zoologists specialize in the study of animals. They often make field trips to remote deserts or mountains to study animals in the wild.

Game wardens enforce fish and wildlife laws. They also make sure that all fishermen and hunters have licenses and don't exceed the allowed catch limits, or fish or hunt out of season.

Marine biologists work to understand the natural equilibrium of the sea. They sometimes work with geologists who study the sea floor to research deep-sea minerals or discovered oil reserves.

Aquaculturists are the gardeners and farmers of the seas and lakes. They cultivate seaweed, fish, and shellfish for sale in stores.

Farmers and ranchers raise and tend livestock. They take good care of their animals, hoping they will earn a fair price when put up for sale.

Working in tourism

Travel agents sell plane, bus, and train tickets to vacationers in downtown shops, in shopping malls, and on the Internet. Ticket sellers also serve travelers in airports and bus and train stations.

At tourist attractions, tour guides take people on visits to galleries and monuments and show them around town. They may also organize the schedules, hotels, and meals so everything will run smoothly for the group.

Workers at information centers give tourists directions and advice on what to do and where to stay.

The tour director welcomes visitors and organizes activities and parties during their stay.

The first farmers and ranchers in the United States sometimes lived in log cabins like this one.

Reconstructed towns that offer a glimpse at life in the Wild West are popular tourist destinations.

The word motel is short for "motor hotel." Motels offer comfortable rooms for tourists traveling by car.

Hotel workers

The receptionist takes reservations and welcomes guests when they arrive. Then the bell hop carries the bags upstairs. The room service waiter brings meals to the room and housekeepers change the sheets and clean the room after the customer has left.

Restaurant workers

Back in the kitchen, the head cook supervises the whole culinary team and prepares the most difficult dishes. Other cooks are in charge of salads, soups, or desserts. Dishwashers scrub the pots and pans and bus people clear the tables when the customers have finished. In cafes, short order cooks prepare fast meals, such as bacon and eggs or hamburgers.

Out in the dining room, the host or hostess welcomes customers, shows them to a table, and gives them menus. The waiter or waitress takes customers' orders and brings the food. The head waiter supervises the wait staff to make sure everything runs smoothly.

Working in fashion
The fashion designer plans a collection of clothes and directs its creation. He or she collaborates with the textile designer who designs original patterns or color mixes for the fabrics. Then they commission a textile printer to print the fabric.

The pattern maker prepares the patterns for each new creation, according to the designer's drawings. All the dimensions are recorded on a computer, which automatically cuts out the pattern pieces from sheets of cardboard.

Models present the new collection to fashion buyers at fashion shows. In the photographer's studio, the makeup artist prepares the models' faces. The models may also pose for photographs destined for fashion magazines.

Iron spearhead

In war and peace, military work has always kept people busy. But the work has changed over the centuries. Soldiers and sailors have the job of defending their country if it is attacked, taking part in military actions all over the world. Soldiers and sailors work for the army, navy, air force, or marines. They do all sorts of jobs: tank driver, fighter pilot, electrician, air traffic controller, doctor, dog trainer, cook, physical education teacher, chaplain, radar operator, photographer, chemist, ballistics engineer, and even military band musician. They all work together to protect our country.

Vanished trades
Many jobs that once existed have disappeared because machines now do the job, or the need for a product or service no longer exists.

The water diviner used a willow branch or two pieces of wire to try to find ground water.

The prospector sifted through muddy river water and tunneled into mountains in search of gold and other precious metals.

The bonepicker followed the buffalo hunters of the 19th century and picked up buffalo bones. These bones were used to make a rich fertilizer.

The mule skinner drove and took care of teams of working mules.

■ Did you know?

Some of the following occupations have disappeared completely, while others are carried on by only a few people.

Lamplighters went through town at dusk with a torch, lighting all the gas lamps in the area.

Home brewers made very strong alcohol by distilling fruits or grains.

Saddlers made and sold harnesses, saddles, bridles, saddle bags, and other leather goods for horses.

Wheelwrights repaired wheels for carts and wagons.

Chandlers used animal fat or beeswax to make candles. They also made soaps and paints and sold them in their shops.

Rope makers wound hemp threads together to form rope.

Cutlers worked silver and iron to produce and repair knives and scissors.

Lace makers wove together very fine threads to make delicate tablecloths, curtains, braids, and collars.

A water wheel inside a mill

Washerwomen cleaned clothes by hand at a wash house or at a river, rubbing their clothes against rocks.

Millers used a millstone to grind wheat and produce flour for bread. They worked, and usually lived, in a mill powered by wind or water.

Tailors cut and sewed clothes to fit customers exactly. Most clothes are now mass-produced in factories.

Weavers made huge rugs with detailed pictures on them to hang in the homes of the wealthy.

A miner works with a pick to dig up valuable stones or minerals. In the 19th century, people worked long hours in coal mines.

Coopers bent strips of heated wood to produce barrels and casks of all shapes and sizes.

Basket makers braided together the stems of cane or rushes to weave mats and baskets.

Working in a mine

Miners dig coal and other metal ores and minerals out of the ground, often in tunnels far below the surface. These days most miners run digging machines. But in the past, they dug with simple hand tools. A pick was used to loosen the ground. Then another miner crouched down in the cramped tunnel to shovel the coal or ore into wagons. Sometimes dynamite was used to break the ground into pieces small enough for the miners to move. Other miners built wooden supports to stop the roof from collapsing. All these jobs were dangerous, and many miners died in accidents.

Working on the railroad
Many new jobs were created with the invention of the train in the 1800s. Today, most of those jobs have disappeared.

At the station before departure, the switchman slid in between the train cars to connect them together. When the time came to slow down, the brakeman left his special compartment at the very back of the train. He ran along the roof from car to car, turning huge handles that jammed the steel wheels. It could take a half mile or more to stop the train.

On a locomotive, the fireman lit the firebox with kerosene and coal. He shoveled in coal bit by bit until the engine had "a full head of steam." This took hours before the engineer could take the train out of the station.

The engineer ran and supervised the train's operation. He made sure that the train and its controls were working properly.

Where the railroad went over roads, the crossing keeper waited in a small building. He or she swung a barrier across to keep wagon drivers and pedestrians off the tracks. It took thousands of workers 12 years to build the Trans-Siberian railway, the world's longest railway. Many of the workers were prisoners. The workers who built the railway across the United States in the 1860s were better paid. It was still back-breaking, dangerous labor.

The first trains were not heated. Porters helped passengers and their bags on and off the train and gave them foot warmers at every station. In luxurious trains like the Orient Express, passengers could dine in style in the dining cars. These trains had their own cooks and waiters.

Working at the market

Fish markets sell fish and shellfish. Before refrigerators and freezers were invented, blocks of ice had to be used to keep the fish fresh.

Fishwives used to walk the streets selling fish from their aprons.

Bakers make and sell bread and pastries. They have been around for a long time; there were hundreds of bakeries in Rome in 100 B.C.

Grocers sell fresh fruits and vegetables at stores or open markets.

At night, the lampman met the train at a stop. He climbed along the train car roofs, lighting the oil lamps on each car.

Creameries once bought milk and cream from farmers. They prepared the milk and cream and made butter and cheese to be sold to their customers in the city. These products are now mass-produced and sold in grocery stores.

Working for the law

Lawyers are trained to understand our many complicated laws. There are many kinds of lawyers. Corporate lawyers specialize in laws that affect large companies. Public defenders are hired by the government to represent people in court who can't afford their own lawyer. Judges preside over the court, and with the jury, decide who is guilty or innocent.

American firefighter

Canadian firefighter

Japanese firefighter

Russian firefighter

Many jobs have their own unique uniforms.

We recognize police officers, flight attendants, and cooks by the special uniform each of them wears on the job.

Can you tell a firefighter from Japan, Canada, Russia, or the United States by his uniform? How are their uniforms different from the ones you are used to seeing?

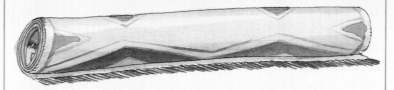

■ Quiz

Can you answer these questions? The answers are at the bottom of the next page.

1. Which of these jobs is the oldest?
   a. Miner
   b. Potter
   c. Farmer

2. What do masons do?
   a. They grow plants in huge pots.
   b. They use stone or brick to build walls or whole buildings.
   c. They work with glass.

3. What was the architect of a medieval cathedral called?
   a. the master planner
   b. the master mason
   c. the entrepreneur

4. A logger spends his time
   a. cutting down trees.
   b. herding goats.
   c. building with wood.

5. What was the artisan called who built and repaired wheels?
   a. the cooper
   b. the wheelwright
   c. the tinker

6. What did Stradivari make?
   a. jazz music
   b. violins
   c. sculptures

7. What does a weaver create?
   a. tapestries, carpets, and rugs
   b. leather objects
   c. combs and brushes

8. What was the peddler?
   a. a professional water carrier
   b. a baggage handler
   c. a traveling salesman

9. What did the draper sell?
   a. exotic spices
   b. fruit and vegetables
   c. cloth

10. Where did Italian merchants travel in the 13th century?
   a. to Africa
   b. to the Far East
   c. to North America

11. What did the apothecary do?
   a. prepared ointments and medicines
   b. built ships
   c. made horseshoes

12. What were the ships of the Spanish merchants called?
   a. cobblers
   b. clippers
   c. galleons

13. What is the machine that prints newspapers called?
   a. the graphics palette
   b. the light table
   c. the press

14. What is the leader of an orchestra called?
   a. the drywaller
   b. the conductor
   c. the cellist

15. **Truck drivers communicate by**
   a. CB radio.
   b. hand signals.
   c. funicular.

16. **The first firefighters were**
   a. people in Chicago.
   b. Dutch water squirts.
   c. Roman slaves.

17. **What does the technical director do?**
   a. switch from camera to camera
   b. organize the props
   c. mark the beginning of every take

18. **What is dubbing?**
   a. making artificial fog
   b. adding background music and sound effects
   c. transferring a film to videotape

19. **Who first used Vitaphone to make talking films?**
   a. Walt Disney
   b. Warner Brothers
   c. Charlie Chaplin

20. **What does a pediatrician do?**
   a. specializes in a baby's growth
   b. looks after your hands and feet
   c. checks your eyesight

■ **True or false?**

Do you know if these statements are correct? The answers are in the column to the right.

1. More than half of the population used to work in the countryside.

2. Tree surgeons and loggers make their living working with trees.

3. In the Middle Ages, the construction of a cathedral often took more than a century.

4. In department stores, you can often haggle over the price of an item with a salesperson.

5. The favorite pastime of the ancient Romans was a night out at the movies.

6. A symphony orchestra is made up of string, percussion, and wind sections.

7. In the past, dentatores treated tooth decay.

8. Computers have made school teachers unnecessary.

9. Astronauts are chosen only for their strength and physical fitness.

10. Airline pilots never fly at night.

11. The producer is responsible for finding the money to make a movie.

12. The draper fixes holes in pots and pans.

13. Firefighters are responsible for more than just putting out fires.

True or False?
Answers:
1. True. Two centuries ago, most people made their living from farming.
2. True. Tree surgeons help keep trees healthy, and loggers cut trees down for lumber and paper pulp.
3. True. It took 157 years to build Notre Dame Cathedral in France. Wars and a lack of money held up construction.
4. False. In department stores, unlike open-air markets, prices are fixed.
5. False. Movies were only invented about 100 years ago.
6. True. There are several different types of instruments in each section.
7. True. Cavities were filled using ground bone.
8. False. Computers are only tools that teachers use to help them teach.
9. False. Astronauts are also chosen for their scientific knowledge.
10. False. Airline pilots fly at night by using radar and other instruments.
11. True. The producer is also usually responsible for choosing a director.
12. False. The draper sells cloth. Tinkers fix holes in pots and pans.
13. True. Firefighters also respond to accidents, help out during natural disasters, and do many other things.

■ Glossary

Apprentice: a young artisan who learns a trade by working for a master in that trade.

Architect: a designer of buildings. The architect draws up plans for a client and then supervises the construction with the various builders.

Blocks and tackle: a pulley system for lifting heavy stones.

Cash crops: crops such as corn or wheat grown to be sold, rather than for the farmer to eat.

CB radio: "Citizen Band" radio that anyone who has a receiver and a microphone may use. Many long distance truck drivers communicate by CB radio.

Cobbler: a maker and mender of shoes.

Crane: a tall, rigid machine for moving heavy material. Modern ports and building sites make extensive use of cranes.

Engineer: there are many kinds of engineers, including mechanical engineers, who design machines; civil engineers, who plan roads and bridges; and electrical engineers, who design electrical systems. The name can also refer to one who operates a train.

Easel: the frame a painter uses to support a canvas while painting.

Enamel: a glass-like coating of metal used to decorate metalwork or jewelry. Any smooth, bright surface decoration is often called enamel.

Environmentalist: someone whose study and work involves caring for the environment and safeguarding the future of all living things.

Factory: large building full of equipment used to manufacture goods, usually in mass quantities. Many factories are run day and night to get the most use out of the expensive equipment.

Hand: an unskilled worker or someone who lends a hand, such as a stage hand, factory hand, or farm hand.

Hawker: in the Middle Ages, a salesperson who walked the streets shouting out the goods he or she had for sale.

Level: a device used for checking the evenness of an object horizontally.

Market: any place where people gather to buy and sell goods of any kind, from fish to fruit to clothes to houses.

Mason: an artisan who builds walls, chimneys, or whole buildings from stone or brick. The stone or brickwork a mason creates is known as masonry.

Miner: a worker who digs into the ground to extract metal ore or coal. In the past, and in poor countries today, miners were manual laborers who worked long hours in difficult conditions. Today the hard work is done by machines which are run by miners.

Nurse: someone who cares for sick people. Modern nurses are highly trained.

Nursery: in gardening, a plot of ground where trees or other plants are grown to be sold to landscapers. Also the place where the plants are sold.

Plumb line: an instrument used to check that an object is even vertically.
Press: a machine that squeezes. Olive presses extract oil from olives; printing presses push paper and inked plates together to print books or newspapers.

Robot: a sophisticated machine that can repeat many actions automatically and with great precision.

Scaffolding: framework of wooden or metal supports put up by builders to give them access to their work.
Shuttle: tool used in weaving to join weft and warp threads.
Souk: large open-air market found in North Africa.

Warp: the long threads stretched tightly the length of a loom. In weaving, the weft threads are passed through the warp threads at right angles to create cloth.
Weft: threads running perpendicular to the warp threads in weaving.
Wholesale: trading in large quantities direct from the distributor rather than a shop. Traders who sell to shops are called wholesalers.

Have you heard these sayings?

"Many hands make light work."
Many workers will get the job done quickly.

"Too many cooks spoil the broth."
If too many people are involved, the job might not be done right.

"A bad workman blames his tools."
A bad worker blames problems on other things instead of taking responsibility for them.

"Idol hands are the devil's workshop."
People with nothing to do often get into trouble.

"All work and no play makes Jack a dull boy."
Everyone needs to relax and enjoy themselves as well as work. There is more to life than just work.

"Make hay while the sun shines."
Take advantage of good conditions to get work done.

"Cut your coat according to your cloth."
Do the best job you can with the tools and materials you have available to you.

"If you pay peanuts, you get monkeys."
Good wages will get good workers.

... or used these expressions?

"To make short work of something"
To tackle a task and finish it quickly

"The tools of the trade"
The things needed to do a specific job

"The tricks of the trade"
The secrets, advantages, and shortcuts learned by working for some time at a specific job

"A Jack of all trades"
Someone who has a variety of different skills

"Business as usual"
When things go on normally, despite some problems

"A labor of love"
A task someone really likes doing

"A Herculean task"
A task that needs strength and persistence to be carried out. In Greek mythology, Hercules was a hero who performed 12 demanding tasks.

The following places may help you learn more about the careers discussed in this book. Many of the places listed here also have sites on the Internet. Visit your local library to learn about more places to visit in your area.

Smithsonian Institution
1000 Jefferson Drive S.W.
Washington, D.C. 20560

Space Center Houston
1601 NASA Road One
Houston, TX 77058

The Science Museum of Minnesota
30 East 10th Street
St. Paul, MN 55101

United States Air Force Museum
1100 Spaatz Street
Wright-Patterson AFB, OH 45433-7102

The Children's Museum
305 Harrison Street
Seattle, WA 98109-4645

San Diego Natural History Museum
1788 El Prado, Balboa Park
P.O. Box 121390
San Diego, CA 92112-1390

National Railroad Museum
2285 South Broadway Street
Green Bay, WI 54304

Rock and Roll Hall of Fame and Museum
One Key Plaza
Cleveland, Ohio 44114

Black Hills Mining Museum
323 West Main Street
P.O. Box 694
Lead, SD 57754

The San Diego Wild Animal Park
15500 San Pasqual Valley Road
Escondido, CA 92027-7017

INDEX

The entries in **bold** refer to whole chapters on the subject.